5

GW01451522

Christian

Poems,

Prose,

Etc.

by
Robert L Doudna

55 Christian Poems, Prose, Etc.

Copyright © 2024 by Robert L Doudna

All rights reserved. No part of this publication may be reproduced, distributed, or transmitted in any form or by any means, including photocopying, recording, or other electronic or mechanical methods, without the prior written permission of the publisher, except in the case of brief quotations embodied in critical reviews and certain other noncommercial uses permitted by copyright law. For permission requests, write to the author, addressed "Attention: Permissions " at

Robert L Doudna
1019 Anzar Road
San Juan Bautista, CA 95045

ISBN: 979-8-9893100-2-9

Cover photos and design by RLD

Poems and Prose are arranged in book alphabetically

A Crown and Three Nails
A Prose, A Praise, A Prayer
A Questioning
Beauty
Brightness
Bubbling Praise
Butterfly
Christmas Eve at my House
Citizen
Clinging to the Vine
Cruisin'
Earth's Face
God Care For Me
Grace
Greatest Gift Given
Healing
Heaven
Heroes
Hidden Blessings
How
I am not Able
I Confessed
I Cry For You
I Have Come
In His Presence
Jesus I Met
Lead Me Lord
Leaning on You
Life, Death
Life
Lord You Are

Etc. is at the end of the book

A Crown and Three Nails

There was a crown, which should have been mine,

not of honor or royalty, but the punishment kind.

It was made of thorns, and I should've bled,

but then Jesus came, and wore it instead.

There were three nails, so long and so sharp,

they were meant for me, my skin to part.

For a death by nails, I was to face,

but Jesus was nailed, up in my place.

The crown and the nails, they were meant for me,

I'd earned them, by my sin, you see.

Then Jesus came, and said, "Let me",

though they were mine, on Him they be.

I was the one, sentenced to die that day,

bearing the crown and the nails, my sin He did pay.

By mounting the cross, His love He did give,

my sentence He took, granting me to live.

A Prose, A Praise, A Prayer

Where is it,

    that my tomorrow doth lie?

Within Your hand,

    oh Lord it doth lie.

Where be my life,

    in all this age?

Within Your bosom,

    oh Lord my life be.

For who is it,

    this life that I live?

It is for You,

    my gracious Savior.

For all of my days,

    all of my tomorrows,

all of my life,

    this that I live,

it is all to You Surrendered,

    all that I possibly can,

all that I have,

    all that I am,

it is to You,

    Jesus my Savior.

???

A Questioning???

So who is it that I,
Should be that would deny,
Those who would follow,
To read not the hollow,
But the full force from within,
What the Spirit speaks I should pen,
Of God by many a way,
Would to His people say,
The words of love and hope,
For the devil lays a slippery slope,
And from that slide downward,
Would cause those to look upward,
To see God's secure arm,
And in that state of alarm,
Reaching out to Him who only,
Can draw back and save the lonely,
To lift up and anchor the drifting,
To enlighten the heart of the unbelieving,
To strengthen the soul of the struggling,
To empower the spirit of those fighting,
To give His people sure assurance,
That from Him only comes deliverance.

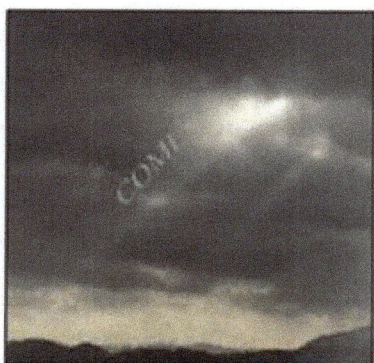

Beauty

The greatest of beauty,

    is unseen,

it is hidden behind,

    a creation in green.

It is yet that,

    which some will see,

when they pass from here,

    so in Heaven they be.

The splendor waits,

    for us to find,

as the beauty of Earth,

    does decline.

The glory of the Lord,

    sat upon His throne,

the beauty of His presence,

    now unknown.

We are here and wait,

    upon that day,

when we're Heaven bound,

    there to stay.

Brightness

In all of the Earth,

    in all of creation,

there is One we look to,

    who holds our fascination.

He is beyond description,

    He is more than we can know,

His face brighter than the sun,

    His clothes whiter than the snow.

He is the light of Heaven,

    the brightness of the universe,

to Him nothing compares,

    and all other deserts.

When we look to His brightness,

    all other becomes dime,

there's nothing in creation,

    that compares to Him.

All beauty around us,

    does fade away,

it leaves us speechless,

    only able to say,

    YOU ALONE ARE GOD.

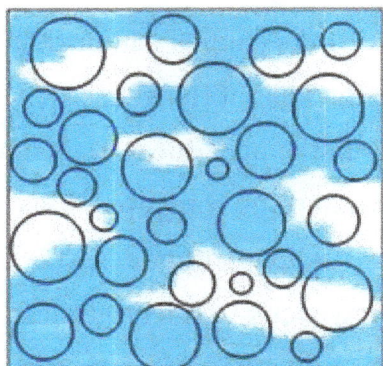

Bubbling Praise

I find praise,

      bubbling from my soul,

it's because of my God,

      who makes me whole.

He blesses my life,

      so greater I'll be,

preparing me for Heaven,

      and eternity.

So I will continue,

      to follow Him,

with God in my life,

      I'm on Heaven's brim.

Now then as He,

      takes me along,

in my heart,

      I will sing His song.

Butterfly

I saw a butterfly go by,
          floating on the wind,
it made a turn, a flutter,
          and then a double spin.
It flies along so gracefully,
          as though no effort spent,
to think for joy and harmony,
          by God, it was sent.
In its wonderful great design,
          our God lacked no skills,
and when it came to us,
          our design He also fills.
We are no mistake,
          that just happened along,
but the result of God's love,
          and to Him we belong.
When He created us,
          He had family in mind,
and reaches out to us,
          that Him we might find.
A more gracious Father,
          He could not be,
He sent Jesus to die for us,
          so from sin we could be free.

Christmas Eve at my House

'Twas the night before Christmas,
      and all through the house,
not a creature was stirring,
      not even a mouse.
But wait a minute now,
      for that is not true,
my kids are all nervous,
      making my house like a zoo!
I send them to bed,
      and reluctant they go,
they want to stay up,
      to see if Santa will show.
Then just when I think,
      they're all asleep in bed,
at the top of the stairs,
      I see the tip of a head.
They'll be up before morning,
      telling me to get up too,
and I'll be so sleepy,
      I'll only find one shoe.
So to bed I take them,
      again one more time,
and coming downstairs,
      I hear the midnight chime.
I hurry and I hustle,
      to do what has to be done,
hoping the work I'm doing,
      will make the next day fun.

↓

Finally I have everything,

    ready to put by the tree,

I move them all around,

    so they're right where they should be.

Now finally I'm done,

    and can get into bed,

so I put on my pajamas,

    and just lay down my head.

Then my kids start yelling,

    all the way down the hall,

they begin jumping on me,

    so I think the bed will fall.

They say, "Come on, get up,

    Christmas morning is here,"

and my night's sleep is over,

    that is certainly clear.

So who said, "nothing was stirring,

    not even a mouse,"

has not spent Christmas Eve,

    with me, at my house!

Citizen

My citizenship is in Heaven,
my life lived in this world.

Like one serving in an embassy,
looking forward to the trip home.

I will serve where I am,
giving attention and honor to those around.

Yet always distinguishing the land that I am from;
by my appearance, my character, and my loyalty,

demonstrating the great place, the great honor,
and the great liberty my homeland offers.

There is no greater liberty,
no greater honor, no greater privilege,
than to represent heaven, and the King thereof.

To the Lord Jesus I have dedicated my life,
to serve in a foreign land,
communicating and demonstrating,
that of the Kingdom of God,

from where I am a citizen.

Clinging to the Vine

As I cling to the Vine,

    allow Your fruit to grow in me.

May they become rich and sweet,

    full of all good things You want me to be.

Let there be love overflowing,
Joy enough to give to the world,
Peace in all situations,
Kindness to overcome evil,
Goodness to act more like You,
Faithfulness to always seek You,
Gentleness to treat others rightly,
And self-control to stand against temptation.

Lord, let Your good fruit grow in me.

Cruisin'

I once thought I was okay,
      living life my simple way,
not much trouble, not much strife,
      it seemed a good and easy life.
For I was cruisin' along great,
      in a simple peaceful state,
then I heard this one man say,
      Jesus is the only way.
Way to where I did wonder,
      this my mind it did ponder,
where was it this guy's goin',
      way to what was he a-showin'.
Cruisin' now was not so easy,
      I even felt a little sleazy,
my peace now it was a slippin',
      my life now began a rippin'.
Now life was not so simple,
      it became a constant ripple,
somethin' inside was a pullin',
      trouble now I was a feelin'.
The easy cruisin' days were gone,
      how would I keep goin' on,
I did need to find that guy,
      if I didn't I felt I'd die.

↓

I followed back how I came,
it pushed me on like a flame,
how would I find him, which way,
what was it more he had to say.
Then I seen him in the crowd,
still sayin' it very loud,
Jesus is the only way,
once again I heard him say.
I needed now to know more,
he said Jesus is the door,
as I listen he explained,
it's by Jesus new life is gained.
He continued on to say,
you can have this life today,
a small prayer is all it takes,
in you a new life Jesus makes.
Ask Him now to be your Lord,
to refuse, you can't afford,
what Jesus has, it is free,
you'll have life for eternity.
I got it then, I understood,
ask Him now is what I should,
Jesus came to my life that day,
now I'm livin' a different way.
Cruisin' again on the go,
a new lane I've come to know,
tellin' others who Jesus is,
has become my whole life's biz.
I thought life was good before,
but now I've found so much more.

Earth's Face

The stars above,
      the moon-lit sea,
how by accident,
      it just can't be.
It is too perfect,
      too laid in place,
all in order,
      in starry space.
Beautiful flowers,
      found all around,
beauty in silence,
      not making a sound.
Trees in order,
      standing together,
in great harmony,
      supporting each other.
Mountains high,
      white clouds above,
seeming to come,
      from someone's love.
How can it be,
      so many will say,
all this formed,
      in an accident way?
Put together well,
      with intent and care,
intended design,
      so wonderfully fair.
↓

Gentle flowing streams,
        and meadows all green,
delight to the eye,
        all that is seen.
The bee, the butterfly,
        a bird flying high,
the porpoise, the whale,
        all make us sigh.
The beauty around,
        we have to admire,
must-of been intent,
        with creative desire.
Men not wise enough,
        accidents not perfect,
not just by chance,
        nor total neglect.
True thought of mind,
        with purpose in place,
put such beauty,
        on this Earth's face.
A kind intent,
        put this together,
must have been God,
        there is no other.
Made so perfect,
        with a gentle touch,
loving us all,
        carrying so much.
God did it all,
        this beauty that be,
Oh, how much He loves,
        both you and me.

God Cares For Me

In my sadness I am secure,

>because I have a God who cares for me.

In my joy I am secure,

>because I have a God who cares for me.

In my troubles I am secure,

>because I have a God who cares for me.

In my peace I am secure,

>because I have a God who cares for me.

No matter where I am or am in, I am secure,

>because I have a God who cares for me.

Grace

In a time long gone by,
           when things were yet unmade,
when there were no stars above,
           and there was no earth below.
When the sun did not shine,
           and the moon did not glow,
there was only One,
           Him I did not know.
He looked from then to now,
           He saw me in my way,
from love who He is,
           He loved me here this day.
He knew me and my troubles,
           He set together a plan,
in His mind I was secure,
           He would keep me by His hand.
He set the stars above,
           He put the earth below,
He made the sun to shine,
           and set the moon to glow,
He put in place the mountains,
           and set the rivers to flow.
He made a beautiful garden,
           He filled with all the trees,
Each to have its own fruit,
           just waiting so to please.

↓

From this creation,
    with foundation now laid,
He gathered a bit of dust,
    from the earth He had made.
He shaped it into man,
    so together they could walk,
among the evening cool,
    and together they could talk.
He gave man a helper,
    one to be his mate,
He gave them the garden,
    and from it they ate.
God gave them all the trees,
    provided food complete,
from one particular tree,
    they were not to eat.
But this man Adam,
    decided not to listen,
and because of that sin,
    from the Garden he was stricken.
This sin set man apart,
    of God who he was made,
to live in separation,
    was now the price he paid.
Through much time that pasted,
    I then came along,
but just as ancestor Adam,
    before God my life was wrong.

↓

My life of sin set me apart,
                from Him who made us all,
for from God's great glory,
                short we all do fall.
But from the beginning,
                God looked forward to me now,
to deliver me from my trouble,
                God alone knew how.
There was another with Him,
                of yet we did not know,
who by His blood our sins,
                could be washed white as snow.
Father God and He the Son,
                had figured out a plan,
that the Son would come,
                redeeming fallen man.
A final sacrifice for sin,
                is what there had to be,
and Jesus the Son came,
                offering Himself on the tree.
This was the plan of grace,
                God had for you and me,
a way to pay the price for sin,
                that we all might be free.
The blood of that sacrifice,
                pays for the sins of man,
now because of that blood,
                before God we can all stand.

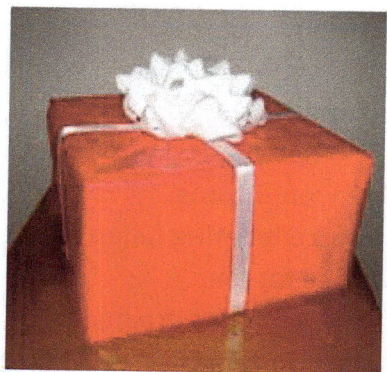

Greatest Gift Given

In the little town of Bethlehem,

        many, many years ago,

in a stable behind an Inn,

        with the stars all aglow.

To a young Jewish girl,

        a babe was born this special night,

and there in the skies above,

        one star shone extra bright.

Animals looked on as admiring,

        this child born among them,

the shepherds came from their meadows,

        looking with wonder upon Him.

Kings came to worship,

        the child of which they had been told,

presenting Him with gracious gifts,

        of frankincense, myrrh, and gold.

This babe would become a man,

        many people would never forget,

He would have an effect on many,

        which has not been equaled yet.

↓

So many would find in Him a hope,

        from despair and strife,

the world would never be the same,

        after this man lived His life.

Yet this man who affected so many,

        never lived to be old,

His life was cut short,

        because He spoke so bold.

And all that was said against Him,

        was nothing but a lie,

born in a stable,

        to a cross He went to die.

This babe Jesus born to die,

        as a gift for us to receive,

that eternal life could be ours,

        if on Him we would believe.

Innocently on the cross He died,

        to pay for all our sin,

from God alone to us,

        has the greatest gift been given.

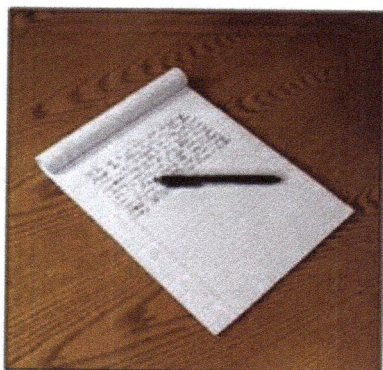

Healing

A pen and a pad,
    what are they to me,
a ray of hope,
    a something I'll be?
My life seems old,
    struggling hard to be known,
is there something I can do,
    that I can say is my own?
Why do I have trouble,
    finding home base with me,
is it myself I don't like,
    or do I just want to be free?
Where can I be in life,
    and at what stage,
why do I write,
    these words on this page?
Are they something inside,
    that wants to come out,
is there something in there,
    that I'd rather shout?
But because of people,
    I think don't want to hear,
to speak a sound,
    I do deadly fear.

↓

That they don't care,
      is what I believe,
so I keep silent,
      and inside quietly grieve.
This pen and this pad,
      they listen to me,
what I have to say,
      and who I care to be.
They do not judge,
      or make strange faces,
they don't make me want to run,
      or to find hiding places.
And now has come,
      my greatest surprise,
these things I believed,
      were nothing but lies.
Many people around me,
      who don't want to hear,
are hiding inside themselves,
      peeking out in fear.
They look strangely at me,
      so they might not be found,
to think this is why,
      I feared to make a sound!
How much at ease,
      we could all be,
if with our lives,
      we could all be free.

↓

Sharing our problems,
  one with another,
listening with loving ears,
  to a sister or a brother.
Why should we live,
  being so tightly bound,
that the depths of our lives,
  be so tightly wound?
It is because,
  of satan you see,
for in our lives,
  he does not want us free.
His lies we've listened to,
  certainly long enough,
it is time to get serious,
  and for us to be tough.
It's not easy at first,
  this I surely know,
but after a while,
  the words will just flow.
Then after you've spoken,
  to ones with loving ears,
and the hurts have been healed,
  by God and warm tears,
then be willing to listen,
  to others with troubles too,
that by your loving ears and God,
  they can be set free just like you.

Heaven

Heaven...,

    what will it be,

when I get there surrounded by it,

    what will I see?

And how will I look at it,

    with these eyes anew,

or will it be with new spiritual eyes,

    Heaven I'll view?

What splendor it surely,

    will have all around,

what glorious things of angels and men,

    will be its sound.

We will all join together,

    to give glory to the King,

and in all of our joy,

    His anthems we'll sing?

Is there anything in this Earth,

    we can compare to its state,

is there any sound here,

    that will not be second rate?

↓

Will the brightest thing of Earth,

    not be dimmer than the dullest there,

will our unity and love not be far beyond,

    that of which we now share?

Can we even imagine,

    what it will be,

that from temptations of sin,

    to be totally free?

As we wait for Heaven,

    can our feeble minds ever understand,

the glorious things of eternity,

    that our Lord God has planned?

What a glorious and wonderful thing,

    that to us our Lord God gives,

and we know we shall surely receive,

    for in our own heart Jesus lives.

Heroes

If I am to have heroes,
    let them be those people of old,
because of how they walked with God,
    and believed what they were told.

Like the man Noah,
    who built a great ship, of God's original design,
even though the rest of men,
    did think he had lost his mind.

And then there was Abraham,
    who not like his family worshiped God alone,
who by God's direction set out for a strange land,
    and made it his home.

Later comes Moses,
    set aside by God, who walked with dedication,
he delivered a great people,
    walked through the sea, and established a nation.

Now there is Elijah,
    God's prophet who confronted those of Baal,
and commanded by God,
    to control clouds and rain, he did not fail.

We must remember Gideon,
    who was the least of the least of the smallest clan,
who believed what God said, and with God's might,
    delivered Israel from the oppressor's hand.

↓

Now there was Daniel, who lived in a foreign land,
      honoring God alone,
defied the king's decree, to not bow and worship another,
      to the lions he was thrown.

So we come now to David, not more than a shepherd boy,
      who God made a king,
who by faith fought Goliath, brought Israel back to God,
      and of God's glory he did sing.

Now we must think of Peter, just a lowly fisherman,
      yet with a faith few of us see,
he walked on water, preached to thousands,
      healed the sick, and set the oppressed free.

Of course, then there was Paul, not the people's choosing,
      yet God used his life,
he traveled the world over, preached the gospel to many,
      and for Jesus lived a life of strife.

These and their like,
      are my heroes to look up to and admire,
to see their faith in God, and their walk in power,
      to my heart they do inspire.

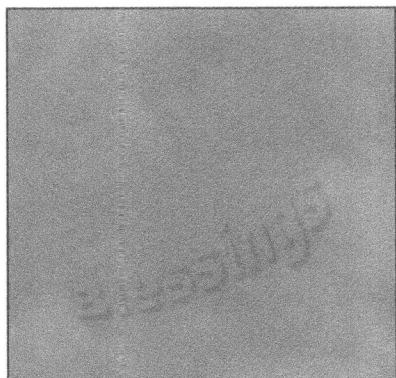

Hidden Blessings

For the auto accident I was not in today,

     thank You Lord, for clearing my way.

For that boiling water that did not fall,

     thank You Lord, for protecting my precious doll.

For that knife today that did not slip,

     thank You Lord, from it my blood did not drip.

For in the storm that tree did not fall,

     thank You Lord, that emergency I did not call.

Thank You Lord, for in all my ways,

     You're always there ahead of me all my days.

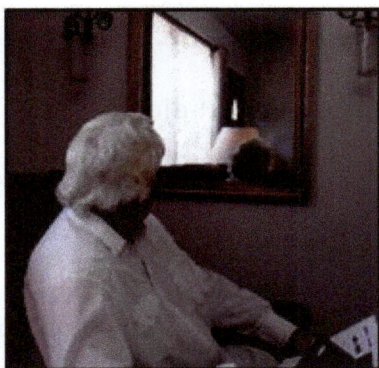

How???

How did I get here,
          so old and so gray,
where did my youth go,
          why didn't it stay?
I didn't even notice,
          the years went by,
they left me sitting here,
          only to sigh.
My future looks short,
          it use to be so long,
somehow it just seems,
          it is all so wrong.
The years I was given,
          so many are all gone,
I need to change my life,
          before another dawn.
I've got to make my life,
          count for something more,
when I die it won't matter,
          if I'm rich or if I'm poor.
Where am I headed,
          I'm not even sure,
it would feel nice,
          to be really secure?
Some say we die and rot,
          and that's the end of that,
done to like a pile of dirt,
          swept under the mat.
↓

There's got to be more to it,
                or it's just such a waste,
it'd be like a great meal,
                that had no taste.
Where did I come from,
                and where am I going,
is there something more,
                I need to be knowing?
I've got to find out,
                I've got'a know the truth,
I should have search for this,
                when I had my youth.
Have I got enough left,
                to this life of mine,
will I find the answer,
                before I cross that final line?
Those people I use to ignore,
                who had something to say,
now I've got to find one,
                feel I can't waste a day.
They seemed in my way,
                when I had things to do,
maybe they had the answer,
                to this truth I pursue.
Where's some of those papers,
                they always left behind,
somewhere, somehow,
                some I've got to find.

↓

Then they didn't matter,
        most I threw away,
maybe in my desk, my car,
        one managed to stay.
Ah, I have found one,
        I must read it through,
it says we all have sinned,
        I realize now that is true.
Is there any hope for me,
        is there a God or a Heaven,
I haven't thought about God,
        since I was eleven?
Now it's time to pay the piper,
        what am I going to do,
I've got to read some more,
        I've got to read it through.
It says I can't do enough,
        to pay my way to Heaven,
I think of all my sinful life,
        from since I was eleven.
What'm I going to do now,
        can I turn it all around,
the way I feel right now,
        I don't dare make a sound?
What plea can I have,
        where is it I'm headed,
if someone gets me to Heaven,
        I'll be deeply indebted.
↓

Read more, read more,
                    got to know more,
it says that with Jesus,
                    He keeps no score.
That if I confess my sins,
                    all He has is free,
a truly repented heart,
                    is all He wants to see.
It says I can be forgiven,
                    for all my sins I've done,
it says Jesus died for me,
                    as God's own Son.
Well I've read it all,
                    to the very end,
now some soul-searching time,
                    I must spend.
I need Jesus to redeem,
                    this tough old soul of mine,
Jesus is my only hope,
                    before I cross that final line.
Those people who came around,
                    I always pushed aside,
They talked about Heaven and God,
                    and Jesus who had died.
They had a future confidence,
                    now I want this too,
ask Jesus into my life,
                    this is what I must do.

I am not Able

I'll give You my all, oh Lord,
        I thank You for all Your love,
I want to You to sing my praise,
        like the song of the morning dove.
I lay my sins before You Lord,
        to forgive them by Your grace,
I'll give You all the praise I can,
        until the day we are face to face.
I look at my life, oh Lord,
        and I see Your great mercy,
I truly thank You Lord,
        for giving to me eternity.
One day I'll be with You Lord,
        there in Heaven on high,
I'll praise and thank You Lord,
        for one day to Heaven I'll fly.
Yet here I'm not able to express,
        all that is surely Your greatness,
my mind cannot comprehend,
        the fullness of all Your glory.
My mouth not able to speak the words,
        great enough to match Your Majesty,
my spirit yearns to praise You Lord,
        with praises my body cannot express.

I Confessed

He was a Holy Man,
   a worker of miracles.
I was a scoundrel,
   a leader of rebels.
He was a kind man,
   one who loved the people.
I thought I did,
   and tried to get them free.
He touched little children,
   and healed the ailing.
The sick and kids were in my way,
   I had important things to do.
He taught about a God,
   who was kind and forgiving.
I followed a way,
   I thought would be liberating.
They struck Him on the cheek,
   so He turned to them the other.
I struck out at them,
   with all the force I could.
They accused Him,
   and He lifted not a hand.
I lifted my hand,
   and was caught in my action.
He said pray for your enemies,
   and do them good.
I hated my enemies,
   and made them dead.
He allowed Himself to be beaten,
   and treated disgracefully.
I was beaten into submission,
   yielding only after a fight.
He was accused,
   of nothing He'd done.
↓

I was accused,
        of all I had done.
He was set to be punished,
        a sentence not deserving.
I was guilty and condemned,
        to be crucified was my fate.
He was innocent,
        and should have been let go.
I was condemned,
        yet I was set free.
They took Him through the streets,
        on His shoulders bearing that cross.
I lurked along in the shadows,
        not wanting to look back.
He stumbled along the way,
        going out the city gate.
I wanted to flee and run,
        yet somehow I turned and followed.
His voice and His look,
        touched people deeply.
Even this hard heart of mine,
        was strangely drawn to Him.
Now He was on that hill,
        being nailed to that cross.
Yet I was the one feeling,
        the piercing of my soul.
He was hung there in shame,
        for all the world to look upon.
I was feeling shame,
        that had never touched me before.
He said to one criminal,
        "Today you will be in paradise."
A yearning was in my soul,
        I wanted to be there also.
On that cross He died,
        and they put Him in the tomb.

↓

Though I was walking,
          all death I felt upon me.
On the third day it was said,
          that He had risen from the dead.
Somehow in my despair,
          a hope rose up within me too.
For forty days it was said,
          He walked among His followers.
Within me something was happening,
          finding I wanted to follow also.
He taught His followers,
          kindness, forgiveness, and love.
These were strange to me,
          I had never known them.
He promised those followers a blessing,
          and one day soon it came.
I heard a strangeness coming,
          from their gathering place.
One of those there,
          spoke of Him who was crucified.
I remembered Him on the cross,
          where I should have died.
His follower said,
          He was the anointed sent to us.
I felt like those around me,
          They said, "What shall we do?"
His follower answered,
          "Repent, repent, and be baptized."
In my heart I felt repentance,
          of my sins, then I confessed.
He who gave His life,
          being put on that cross.
Now changes that death in me,
          to life and I'm set free.

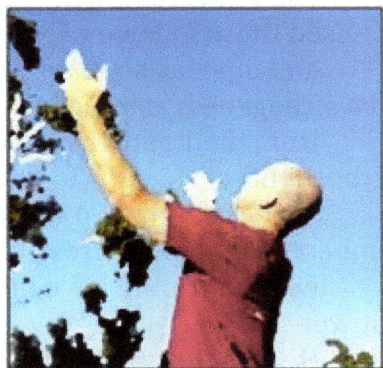

I Cry For You

I reach out,
  to find You there,
it is I who stand,
  waiting here.
There is a tearing,
  inside of me,
desiring close to You,
  that I can be.
A longing within,
  that stirs my soul,
to move close to You,
  for You to behold.
I strive and reach,
  to touch Your hem,
to be close to You,
  the heavenly Lamb.
To touch You Lord,
  my soul crys out,
such a yearning,
  I feel to shout.
The crying is deep,
  desire so strong,
with all of my soul,
  for You I long.
Wanting to touch,
  wanting to know,
to know Your love,
  to me You would show.
I cry and long,
  to feel Your touch,
that closeness to feel,
  Oh so much.
Crying to You,
  in closeness to be,
joy of joys,
  that would be to me.

"I Have Come"

Listen, children,
> to what I say,
listen, children,
> to what I say.
I have come among you,
> as a man this day,
to correct an error,
> of Adam's way.
He gave you sin,
> which only death can pay,
severing your lives,
> from God's holy way.
I have come now,
> your lives to restore,
but a price must be paid,
> for sin God does abhor.
God has chosen Me,
> His Son to do this task,
yes, even My very life,
> My death on the cross He does ask.
Now don't be alarmed,
> I'm not really going away,
I must deal with death,
> and come back the third day.
Once I have died,
> the penalty is paid,
in the giving of My life,
> the sacrifice has been made.

In His Presence

As sky surrounds the meadow,

        so God's love surrounds me.

It is as the morning mist,

        that saturates the tree.

His love is never-ending,

        it is far more than I can see.

It will carry me into Heaven,

        where in His presence I'll ever be.

Jesus I Met

Jesus I met, and we talked one day,

He told me of life, the heavenly way.

I asked Him what thing, it was I could do,

to gain this life, from heaven anew.

He said to me, with a sincerity true,

"There is nothing, but nothing, that you can do."

But then He told me, there was a way,

only He could do it, but what He wouldn't say.

I waited and I wondered, what it could be,

this thing that Jesus, would do for me.

Would He work a miracle, or give me a word,

I wanted to see heaven, from all that I had heard?

Then to my shock, and to my surprise,

they arrested Him, accusing Him, with nothing but lies.

They shouted out, and yelled out, Crucify, Crucify!

Oh, I pleaded and I asked them, Why oh Why?

↓

I said they couldn't, He was an innocent man,

but I seemed the least heard, in all of the land.

Oh, my hope of heaven, was now gone for sure,

this tragedy seemed more, than I could endure.

That special thing, He was going to do for me,

now He couldn't, and heaven I would never see.

As I stood in the crowd, they put up the cross,

my heart was breaking, Oh what a loss!

Then the soldiers began, to bring Him near,

before, I had hope, but now only fear.

With nails and hammers, the soldiers they stood,

waiting to nail, His flesh to the wood.

Then He stopped at the cross, where I could see,

raising His arm, He pointed right at me.

Then with a gentle, and loving voice too,

He said to me, "This I do for you."

Lead Me Lord

Lord, lead me forward,

    show me the way,

take me by the hand,

    so on Your path I'll stay.

Lord, open my eyes,

    to what You want me to see,

help me to find how,

    You would have me to be.

Turn me away from where,

    my flesh wants to take me,

give me the strength to resist,

    so that I can be free.

I want to serve You,

    and follow Your way,

Oh Lord, forgive my sins,

    I've committed today.

↓

My life is in Your hands,

       as it always will be,

I have given You my heart,

       and all that is me.

You are my God,

       and in You I trust,

You've created me,

       from the dust.

On the cross You redeemed me,

       saving me from hell,

and I look forward to the day,

       I hear that heavenly bell.

Until then Lord,

       a true effort I'll make,

and the path as the world goes,

       I will not take.

Following You is what,

       I want to do,

help me stay close,

       and to You always true.

Leaning On You

As I lean on You Lord,
my life becomes easier,
my struggle softer,
and my time freer.

As I lean on You Lord,
I have strength for the battles,
purpose in the perseverance,
victory with the victorious.

As I lean on You Lord,
truth becomes more clear,
knowledge of You brighter,
eternal understanding greater.

As I lean on You Lord,
my way is secure,
my destiny confirmed,
my eternal place sure.

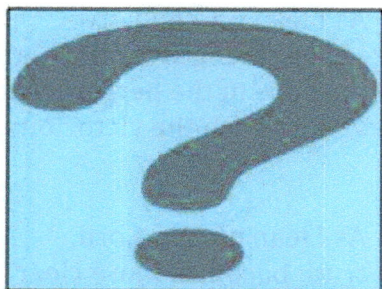

Life? Death?

What is life if it is not life,
what is death if it is not death?
How can we go on,
where is it we are going?
Do we know?
This is the question that has to be answered.

Can we carelessly keep going forward,
not knowing where we are headed?
Laying down tracks to nowhere,
where will we be when we get there?
Do we know?
This is the question that has to be answered.

Our lives ruined,
our past extinguished,
our future short,
our lives nearly over.
What is it we know?
This is the question that has to be answered.

What is life if it is not life,
what is death if it is not death?
Life is continued life if we know God,
death is continued death if we know not God.
God is life and gives it to all who come to Him,
without God, not coming to God,
is only continuing in death.

*"God loved the world so much that he gave his only Son,
that whoever believes in him will not perish but have eternal
life."* John 3:16

Life

The current of our lives,

       as it flows through the years,

the high points, the low points,

       and those times of tears.

The great times, the joyous times,

       those happy places in life,

all those things that fill our minds,

       memories of joy and memories of strife.

They all come together,

       they affect the way we live,

the memories that affect us most,

       are ones most attention we give.

To focus on the strife of life,

       more strife there'll be to come,

to focus on the joys of life,

       more joys there'll be to come.

Whether joy or strife we think most,

       it is that which affect how we be,

which it is we think of most,

       that will be the most we see.

We have a choice to make in life,

       that of which it can be,

no matter how it may come,

       which is it most you choose to see?

Lord You Are

Lord You are, that which always has been,

    and Yes You are, the One who will always be.

You have brought about, all we know and see,

    it is You oh Lord, that has made even me.

All that is, is because of You,

    You are what, all this is about.

The jet flying high, a tree moved by the breeze,

    the gentle ocean swells, a bird in its migrating route.

Man's accomplishments, many all around,

    many things that are, in this busy world we see.

Much activity sure, we do take credit for,

    much we have done, by who it is we be.

Yet our eyes, must not stop there,

    it is not us, who has made us great.

There is a God, who has created all,

    no matter what we've done, in Him does lie our fate.

He is what, this world is about,

    all answers to Him, of all that be.

How little we do, compared to what He has done,

    the sun, the moon, the stars that we see.

Even what we do, is because of Him,

    He permeates the world, it's Him it is about.

Seeing all He has done, all that He has made us to be,

    it is to Him we thank, and His praise to shout.

Me

My greater life,

        I do not see,

when I look in the mirror,

        what I see is not me.

That is my tent,

        where I dwell for now,

one day I will depart,

        before the Lord to bow.

So I continue on,

        and wait my day,

to be of service to Him,

        as here I stay.

In my Spirit to grow,

        in service to Him,

as I wait here,

        upon Heaven's brim.

What I see in the mirror,

        it is not me,

when I arrive in Heaven,

        I will know what I be.

Memories

The hour that was,
      and is no more,
it is a ship that sailed,
      to a distant shore.
There is no return,
      to come back again,
that remembered appearance,
      will have to stand.
The memory will do,
      to fill the heart,
to bring a joy,
      that it will start.
To lay on the mind,
      a beautiful scene,
a day to remember,
      so right and so clean.
A joy we had,
      that will not fade,
one that joint - ly,
      by us was made.
There will always be a place,
      for those thoughts,
many to remember,
      for there were lots.
That ship may not return,
      to this shore,
but the memories of them,
      will continue to soar.

My Dry Eyes

Oh Lord, my eyes have been so dry,

Oh Lord, my eyes have been so dry,

so dry for so long, oh so long.

Oh Lord, I need rivers to flow,

to flow from my eyes,

Oh Lord, to flow.

For gladness and sadness,

to know what You have done for me,

to know what I have done to You.

To recognize my sinfulness,

to recognize Your gentleness,

to know the weight of my sins,

to know the depth of Your grace.

Oh Lord, my eyes have been so dry,

Oh Lord, my eyes have been so dry,

So dry for so long, oh so long.

Oh Lord, I need rivers to flow,

to flow from my eyes,

from sadness and gladness,

Oh Lord to flow, Oh Lord to flow.

Prayer on the Way to Emmaus

As we walk to Emmaus,
> would You hear what I say,

as we go along,
> would close to me You stay?

Walk with me Lord,
> walk along as I go,

speak to me as we walk,
> and let Your words flow.

Speak to me Lord,
> make Your words clear,

please make them bright,
> let them ward off my fear.

Let them bring me to praise,
> and to worship You,

where Your name becomes,
> my pure delight so true.

Let my joy in You,
> cause me to be strong,

let my prayer and worship,
> carry me along.

Let victory come,
> as praise to You I give,

may Your name be glorified,
> by the way that I live.

May Your Kingdom come,
> and may Your will be done.

Amen.

Secure in Jesus

Through the valley with Jesus,

        a savior not at all weak,

one who brings us strength and joy,

        when our situation seems so bleak.

He never turns away from us,

        He never leaves our side,

over rocky areas He carries us,

        like a ship by the rising tide.

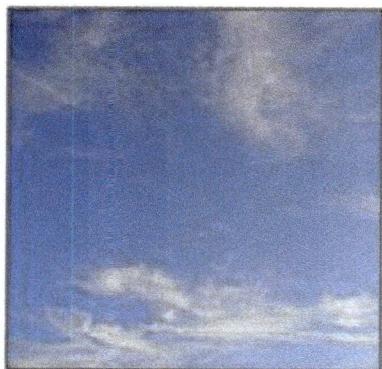

Someone Flew Away Today

Someone I knew,

       flew away today,

they flew to heaven,

       and here I stay.

One day I will follow,

       and be with them again,

they're with Jesus,

       who is our true friend.

When they were here,

       the real person was inside,

the part I saw,

       would someday die.

The real person lives on,

       and to Heaven they flew,

the day is coming,

       that I'll fly there too.

They flew away,

       and left all tears behind,

beauty, peace, and joy,

       is now what they find.

↓

Sorrow and pain,

        they also left here,

there's none of that in heaven,

        not even fear.

They have no more burdens,

        or carry heavy loads,

and all of their ways,

        are now easy roads.

This life here,

        is but a beginning,

but real life starts,

        at this life's ending.

Someone I knew,

        flew away today.

Sometimes Life is Rough

Sometimes life is rough,

    and getting through the day is tough.

It presses hard against us,

    feeling we are in the dust.

We become weary and worn,

    it becomes an agony as a foot with a thorn.

As we turn to God in our prayer,

    opening our heart to Him our troubles we share.

He listens to us like no other,

    more than a sister or a brother.

He acts on our part so we are blessed,

    He chooses the route from our troubles

        that for us will be best.

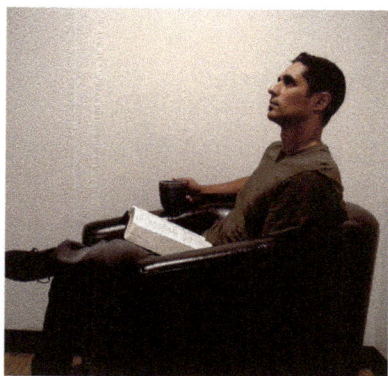

Take My Life

Take my day,

    and turn it Your way,

        be all that moves in me.

My life is yours,

    it belongs to You,

        Order it today.

Let not troubles,

    or fear to enter in,

Be Lord of my life,

    and all that I be,

So that I will flow,

    and always be free.

The Light

There is a light,

        coming from above,

an unseen light,

        yet full of love.

It shines bright on man,

        it comes with force,

it's the love of God,

        that is its source.

Penetrating every heart,

        deeply going far within,

cutting through the darkness,

        that there has been.

It shines brightly,

        to call to us,

we started with Him,

        making us from dust.

We followed our own,

        and went astray,

we did not look,

        to find His way.

↓

Now in despair,

        we struggle along,

we find life hard,

        something seems wrong.

It is that light,

        trying to reach our heart,

if only we'd see,

        we'd have a new start.

Jesus would come in,

        giving us the light,

darkness would be gone,

        life would be so bright.

Why in darkness,

        did we stay,

when clearly Jesus,

        is the way?

The Night, The Darkness

How deep the night,
      how mellow the darkness,
not at all,
      what it used to be.
There was a time,
      that all I knew,
was day after day,
      fear after fear.
There was no release,
      there was no shelter,
none could help,
      none could touch,
the deep, deep, fear,
      in the bottom of my soul.
I longed to be free,
      longed to be lifted out,
I searched, I hunted,
      I looked and I looked.
Fear upon fear,
      darkness upon darkness,
there was no help,
      none to lift me out.
Then I heard,
      "Jesus is savior,
He can help,
      where none other can."

↓

That's what I needed,
        what none other can,
one to lift me up,
        out of the darkness of my soul.
The night and its darkness,
        crushing in upon me,
the night's darkness,
        weighing upon the darkness within.
It was torture,
        it was torment,
I needed help,
        someone to save me.
Maybe this Jesus,
        maybe He can,
I prayed to Him,
        I gave my life to Him.
A light entered,
        my deep darkness,
that light drove,
        that darkness from me.
With the darkness now gone,
        and the new light within,
that light Jesus gave me,
        that liberated my soul.
Now the night is sweet,
        and its darkness mellow.
no more fear,
        nor darkness within.
Nothing but light,
        in the darkest of night,
Jesus has lifted me out,
        of the deep darkness I was in.

The Old Man and His Clock

That old clock,

      round and round it goes,

it never stammers, or stutters,

      or even slows.

I really try to keep up,

      and I think I'm go'n fast,

but when the race is o'er, that old clock has won,

      and I came in last.

This battle, it goes on,

      day after day,

to beat that old clock,

      there just seems no way.

No matter how long it runs,

      it never gets weary,

and as I watch it go round,

      I'm beginning to get leery.

It seems that over the years,

      it has surely speeded up,

for I get less work done,

      and find my coffee cold in my cup.

↓

The work I'm a-do'n,

        is the same I've done before,

yet that old clock,

        it goes round twice again more.

No matter how much I hurry,

        that old clock's always ahead,

and before I've done a day's work,

        it's already time for bed.

Now I know I'm still work'n,

        at that same fast pace,

so how is it then,

        that I can be lose'n this race?

It couldn't be me,

        I know I'm not slower,

and I'm go'na shoot that old clock,

        before it's all o'er.

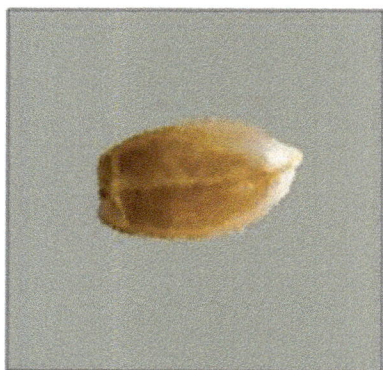

The Seed

What is it we,
>> put in the ground,
that brings new life,
>> sturdy and sound?
How is it the Oak tree,
>> grows so tall,
and despite strong winds,
>> it doesn't fall?
In what direction around us,
>> can we not see,
some life in a plant,
>> that has come to be?
Who has ordered,
>> this power of the seed,
to spring forth against resistance,
>> to do its deed?
The Great Creator,
>> has made this plan,
to support the earth,
>> with that work of His hand.
It fills our stomachs,
>> and shads our head,
it supports our sitting,
>> and makes soft our bed.
It feeds our livestock,
>> and helps build our house,
wild creates feed on it,
>> even the mouse.

↓

What a marvelous thing,
            God has created for us,
does its great work,
            with little toil or fuss.
Could there be anything greater,
            for a seed to do,
that it dies in the earth,
            and springs up anew?
Could it be in God's,
            great eternal plan,
its greatest purpose was not,
            for what we hold in our hand.
It was a much deeper thing,
            God wanted us to see,
He needed to show us,
            how it could be.
A great eternal truth,
            He wanted to explain,
of how things work,
            in His eternal reign.
Life can only survive,
            without the stain of sin,
and something has to change,
            what our life has been.
We need to grow anew,
            sturdy and strong,
we have to do something,
            about what we've done wrong.

↓

But there's nothing we can do,
        that will wipe it away,
those stains of sin,
        we find in us today.
It does seem hopeless,
        to receive eternal life,
to earn it we cannot,
        even with much work and strife.
But God knew our need,
        and provided a way,
for that came Jesus,
        but not to stay.
Jesus taught us and told us,
        what we need to do,
to believe in Him,
        would give us life anew.
As a seed to come anew,
        its own death it will take,
Jesus by His death,
        a way for us He did make.
As we yield ourselves to Him,
        we are who sprout up anew,
accepting Him as Lord,
        in us a new life grew.
Now we walk daily,
        in the strength of His life,
we find as we live in Him,
        there is now less strife.
Jesus renews us,
        like a strong growing tree,
through His death for our sins,
        we have grown anew and are free.

The Sun It Rises

The sun it rises,
   as the Lord God ordered,
putting away night,
   and brings us the day.
We see His blessings,
   very clearly before us,
it gives us sure joy,
   while going our way.
Our day it comes full,
   as God fills it with good,
and it is complete,
   supplying all we need.
We go through our day,
   blessed with His covering,
with troubles removed,
   in safety He does lead.

The Trees

We are the trees,
       who hold tight to the Earth,
it is God by His Word,
       who gave us birth.
Some of us are mighty,
       and some of us small,
some of us are broad,
       and some of us tall.
Some of us are large and wide,
       and cover the ground,
when the wind touches our leaves,
       we make a beautiful sound.
Some of us have wide leaves,
       to give man shade,
some of our leaves are thin,
       and more like a blade.
Some of us are very old,
       seeming never to die,
some grow tall and pointed,
       seeming to pierce the sky.
For us, our God given job,
       is to produce the seed,
and for some of us,
       it is to animal and man to feed.

↓

Man has used us,
>to build a house, a bridge, a ride,

with us he has built huge ships,
>that ride over the tide.

Carpenters love us,
>making some wonderfully great things,

from us is built the steeple,
>where the church bell rings.

We trees have been here,
>since nearly time began,

we were standing there tall,
>when God did make man.

We were part of the garden,
>where Adam was to be,

Adam and Eve were among us,
>very blessed and free.

We seen satan convinced Eve,
>to take the forbidden fruit,

then Eve did give to Adam,
>and he did follow suit.

We were there when the angle,
>took his place at the gate,

being cast out of the garden,
>became man's fate.

We watched man go with God,
>and then go from God,

by his sweat to till the ground,
>and to bust the clod.

↓

It was from one of us,
        that a branch did lie,
that in the hand of Cain,
        as a club Able did die.
We observed man through the ages,
        who couldn't live God's way,
and man's hard heart of sin,
        was what ruled his day.
Standing there tall we many times shuttered,
        at what all we saw man to do,
we could see man's denial,
        of God's way was surely true.
We stood by watching man,
        for all those years,
causing us great sorrow,
        in the morning dew we shed our tears.
Then one of our brothers,
        had a most honorable job,
in the midst of a crowd,
        looking more like a mob.
He had a duty to perform,
        as he stood up straight,
on no tree would he ever,
        wish such a fate.
What he had to do,
        did make him sad,
the state of man,
        had gone nearly mad.

↓

For on him they hung,
              the Lord of all,
who came to Earth to die,
              because of man's fall.
It was on him that day,
              that the Lord did die,
as the Lord's blood ran down,
              all he could do was sigh.
Yet was victory that day,
              in this tragedy,
for by our Lord's blood,
              man now could plea.
Now man could ask God,
              to forgive his way,
and by Jesus' blood,
              in God's grace he could stay.
We trees were able to help,
              with God's great plan,
for Jesus to die on the cross,
              redeeming sinful man.
Now in the morning dew,
              it's our tears of joy that fall,
because now Jesus has become,
              LORD OF ALL.

Thirsting

My heart yearns for Your touch,
my soul thirsts within me,
it is You my God that I search for,
it is You I seek.
How Your mercies pour forth upon me,
how Your love surrounds me,
who is it that can say You are unkind,
who can say You are unjust?
What is there of man that can satisfy me,
what is there of this world that can give me peace,
my heart is laid out before You,
it is You only that I seek.
None other will satisfy me,
none can take Your place,
my life is before You,
my will surrendered to You.
You are the God I seek,
You are the God,
that fills this thirsting of my soul.

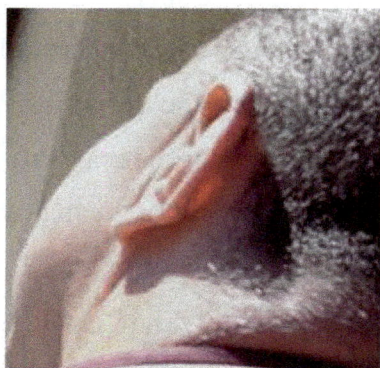

To Hear

In my closet to God I pray,

  I tell Him about my life this day.

To hear Him speak I do desire,

  that would set my heart afire.

To hear Him speak I do wait,

  and when He does it won't be late.

To hear Him speak I know I'll hear,

  for He is not far but always near.

To hear Him speak will feed my soul,

  and stop the world from taking its toll.

To hear Him speak is what I live for,

  to be close to Him more and more.

To hear Him speak my ear I bend,

  and then He tells me that I'm His friend.

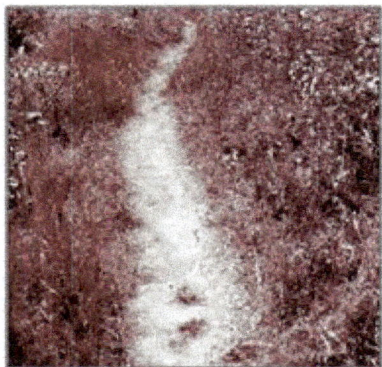

Walk With Me

Lord, would you come,

       and walk with me today,

would You talk with me,

       as I go along my way?

Would You come along,

       and be my friend,

so that some precious time,

       we could spend?

Tell me about Yourself,

       so I can come to know,

who You are to me,

       and my spirit then will grow.

In my heart deep,

       place a song to stay,

so a soul full of joy,

       I'll have as I go my way.

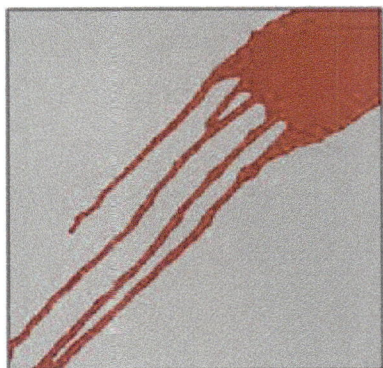

WAR???

War, war, war, war,
why is there war?
What is it all for?
For what does man find,
that he makes another blind,
that he cripples one for life,
that he makes one's blood run red,
and leaves another face down dead?
Why is there war,
What can be the cause?
Is a man so worthless,
that his life is cast aside?
Does he have so little value,
that he is snuffed out like a candle flame?
Does he who strikes out not know,
that on him will come the same?
War, war, war, war,
why is there war?

P.S. Even though I know the
answer, I still have to ask
the question.

What Can I Do?

I cannot love Him,
until His love I know.
I cannot have faith in Him,
until His faith I know.
I cannot know my sonship,
until His Sonship I know.
I cannot have true peace,
until His peace I know.
I cannot have true joy,
until His joy I know.
I cannot know acceptance,
until His acceptance of me I know.

Complete happiness can only come,
when I know all that He is toward me.
I can only have all of this, by becoming like Him.
That He lives fully in me, by His power to be there,
not by any of my power, to put Him there.
I am powerless, to serve Him in any way,
or to gain anything from Him,
it is His power, that does it all.

↓

The only thing I can do,

surrender forsaking all of self,

remove my own efforts from out of His way,

open the door and let Him in,

that He may get to work,

and to make sure I give Him,

the key to every room of my life.

As He works and we stay out of the way,

the job will be done,

complete with the strength,

to withstand the storms.

When all that we have,

and all we are, are His,

what we become,

is like Him.

What I've Become

What is this,
          that I've become,
the slave of one,
          who calls me son?
This one who loves,
          and calls so much,
to reach our souls,
          our hearts to touch.
He called me close,
          my heart to see,
to help me to,
          my fullness be.
I was well,
          all on my own,
until my sin-
          fullness was shown.
It did lay,
          in darkness hidden,
but in the light,
          it was forbidden.
It was shown to me,
          that I might see,
that where I was headed,
          in hell I'd be.

↓

There seemed no hope,
              no way out,
the thought of it all,
              made me shout.
"Where am I going,
              what will my end be,
can nothing be done,
              to yet redeem me?
Are my sins locked in,
              can they not be removed,
if one could, would he not,
              have all my gratitude?"
I searched my soul,
              I searched my heart,
my sins were stuck there,
              like a dart.
Then one came,
              which I did not know,
the way to freedom,
              He did show.
Not by my will,
              could I brake this bind,
surrender was my hope,
              that I did find.
One paid my price,
              so long ago,
it was done by His will,
              as His blood did flow.

↓

His name is Jesus,
     who did die for me,
my sinful debt He paid,
     that I'd be free.
God sent Jesus,
     to pay my price,
it was Jesus who,
     God did sacrifice.
My debt was paid,
     and I was bought,
but not to be the slave,
     that I had thought.
For God the Father,
     has called me son,
freer than this,
     there can be none.
God's love for me,
     provides all I need,
by His grace through Jesus,
     I had been freed.
For all my sins,
     I owed no longer,
and each day spiritually,
     I am stronger.
Now I am part,
     of that eternal family,
the Father, the Son,
     the Spirit, and me.

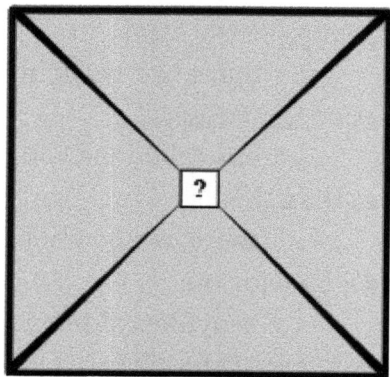

Whats'a gon'a be

We ain't none,
        gon'a last forever,
we ain't none,
        that die'n won't be.
All our time,
        it's a pass'n,
it's all short,
        how little we see.
What's a happ'n,
        when this life's done,
what'a I know'n,
        when this shows over?
Can I be sure,
        there ain't no more,
will it just be,
        I'm push'n up clover?
What if it ain't,
        when this body's dead,
yet I'm still know'n,
        in some space or form?
Where my at,
        what's a happ'n,
answers I'm need'n,
        think'n's like a storm?
My head's a spin'n,
        confusion's consum'n,
I got'a know,
        'fur this body's done.
↓

Could a God there be,
            so many say no,
is it possible,
            Jesus is the Son?
I've heard much,
            what said He did,
it's been told,
            He died on a cross.
And all our sins,
            have done us in,
and without His blood,
            we'r all at a loss.
Could it be,
            a judge I'll face,
did Jesus die,
            also for me?
Would my sins,
            by what He done,
be all paid for,
            and heaven I'd see?
Got'a get this right,
            no time to waste,
Jesus are You real,
            I'm com'n to You.
Forgive my sins,
            wash me clean,
if heaven's real,
            I want'a come too.

Who am I Lord?

Who am I to know Your will?
Who am I to see Your face?
Who am I to know Your ways?
Who am I to love Your people?
Who am I to see Your ways?
Who am I that You would,
bestow on me this knowledge?
How can it be that on me,
You would have this favor?
How can it be that to me,
You would give Your mercy?
How can it be that to me,
You would give Your grace?
What am I, that You would love me?
It is only by Your positive thoughts
toward me that any of this can be.
All that I can be is only possible,
when I surrender to You my all,
to what You want to do in me,
that these things can be.
Amen.

Who Thinks Well of Me

Even if none other,

       thinks well of me,

Lord Jesus in Your heart,

       I will always be.

From Heaven You,

       were willing to leave,

that for this soul of mine,

       You would retrieve.

I was lost unaware,

       of where I was headed,

now my life to You,

       I am fully indebted.

My sin it was,

       surely the source,

to hell and death,

       was my course.

There was no way out,

       I could earn or gain,

there was nothing waiting,

       except more pain.

↓

Jesus You whispered,

        into my heart,

that from my sins,

        I could depart.

That if I accept You,

        into my life,

You would free me,

        from my struggle and strife.

You came into my heart,

        cleansing all of me,

now from all my sins,

        I am set free.

You have made a place,

        in heaven just for me,

and in that day,

        all Your glory I'll see.

You reached out to me,

        when none other cared,

and all my sins,

        You took and bared.

Even if none other,

        thinks well of me,

Lord Jesus in Your heart,

        I will always be.

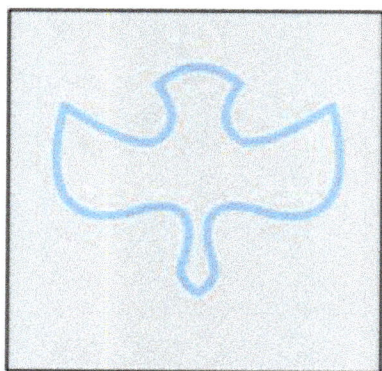

Work in Me

Holy Spirit come,

        work in me today,

Whisper in my heart,

        what God has t'say.

Guide me as I go,

        and help me see the need,

In those who walk beside me,

        to plant some gospel seed.

Remind me of the things,

        Jesus said to do,

Not thinking worldly thoughts,

        but only what is true.

Show me in my Bible,

        of what I should read,

So on the Holy Word,

        my soul may richly feed.

Etc.

As the morning mist settles
in the valley of the mountains,
so does God's peace
settle upon my soul.

It is not so much as what we do for Him,
as it is what we let Him do through us.

We should not focus
on our failures,
but on His successes.

Once God makes us know
we are little He can make us big.
He cannot make us big
until we know we are little.

Youth has gone from me,
and I wasn't done with it yet!

The fullness of the universe
as compared to the Earth,
is the thoughts of God
compared to what I know.

The fullness of the universe
as compared to the Earth,
is the thoughts of God
compared to what I know.

An approach in hast,
usually creates waste.

The thoughts in my mind,
are like money in a piggy bank,
They're secure, they're valuable,
and they're very hard to get out!

Don't limit heavenly activities
by earthly understandings.

Culture does not change
the value of God's Word.
God's Word changes
the value of the culture.

The 'whys' are not so important
when we know the 'Who' we belong to.

Humanity is sometimes too busy
patting humanity on the back
to give God the glory
for the things He has done.

We are victims of time,
it is always chasing us,
or holding us back!

Perfect people are not
accepted into heaven,
only broken ones.

We are not blessed by God
because we are good,
we are blessed by God
because He is good.

In pursuit of God
we will always be knowing more
but never knowing all.

Better to be no one of importance and know it,
than to think we are someone important
not knowing we aren't.

The steps into old age
is not always a pleasant walk.

As Jesus's blood ran down
we were being lifted up.

Mistakes are the mark of progress,
If nothing was done there'd be no mistakes!

Hard times are not a bad thing,
they force us to be together,
because none of us can afford
to be independent in them.

To become more than I was,
I have to become less than I am.

I don't have time
to maintain these regrets.

When age has caught up with you,
and you judge time by
what you have got done,
then evening comes
when it is still morning.

Sometimes we don't know
how sweet our fruit is,
until someone else tastes it.

Grace is a free gift with no
payment in return possible.

Having happiness,
is not by what you have,
It is by Who has you.

Life has this thing about sneaking by
without telling us about it.

There may be heroes in God's kingdom,
but there are no celebrities.

God's faithfulness is not
related to how 'we think'
or how 'we feel,'
it is related to
what He has said.

Hidden Blessings:
I didn't know they didn't happen,
the troubles that I never saw.

Did God create a beautiful place
for us to enjoy,   OR
did He create us to enjoy
the beautiful place He created?

The hardest work I have ever done
is when God says 'wait,'
and the most difficult skill
I have had to accomplish is 'patience.'

When it is, we fully know who we are not,
it is then we begin to know who fully God is.

There is more truth in awkward words
than there are in smooth sayings.

Don't allow the failures of the past
to ruin the victories of the future.

I would rather be thought a fool
because of what I believe,
than to be a fool
because of what I do not believe.

It is a good thing,
that wisdom comes with age,
because everything else leaves!!

Beauty is written on the face of the earth,
without knowing the author it has little lasting value.

You don't have to work
at making room
in your life for God,
God has made room
in His life for you.

Jesus has moved me:
'From a place I couldn't get out of
to a place I couldn't get into.'

Nature dealt me a cruel fate
if it allowed me to be born,
then when I die it is all over.

The statement said by God 'I AM'
is the shortest statement,
and the fullest statement.

Peace has to come to the soul
before joy can live in the heart.

Regrets do not take me forward
they only tie me down to the past.

Submission is greater
than any performance.

The words the hardest to chew
and the one we choke on most
are the words we've spoken ourselves.

The thoughts in my mind,
are like a bird that flies in
through an open window of a house,
flutters around a moment,
and then out and is gone.

As we begin to judge other men
and we start to separate from them,
soon we find we must separate
from that one who is in the mirror.

Milton Keynes UK
Ingram Content Group UK Ltd.
UKHW021959141024
449705UK00009B/417

9 798989 310029